Leadership for Sustainability and Change

T0298597

Cynthia Scott

Core Faculty, Presidio Graduate School
Founder, Changeworks Labs e:
cynthia@cynthia-scott.com
http://cynthia-scott.com
http://changeworkslab.com

Tammy Esteves

Assistant Professor, Troy University
Adjunct Faculty, Presidio Graduate School
tammy.esteves@gmail.com
@tlesteves
http://tammyesteves.me

First published in 2013 by Dō Sustainability

87 Lonsdale Road, Oxford OX2 7ET, UK

ISBN 978-1-909293-70-0 (eBook-ePub)

ISBN 978-1-909293-71-7 (eBook-PDF)

ISBN 978-1-909293-69-4 (Paperback)

A catalogue record for this title is available from the British Library.

Dō Sustainability strives for net positive social and environmental impact. See our sustainability policy at **www.dosustainability.com**.

Page design and typesetting by Alison Rayner

Cover by Becky Chilcott

For further information on Dō Sustainability, visit our website: **www.dosustainability.com**

DōShorts

Dō Sustainability is the publisher of **DōShorts**: short, high-value ebooks that distil sustainability best practice and business insights for busy, results-driven professionals. Each DōShort can be read in 90 minutes.

New and forthcoming DōShorts – stay up to date

We publish 3 to 5 new DōShorts each month. The best way to keep up to date? Sign up to our short, monthly newsletter. Go to **www.dosustainability.com/newsletter** to sign up to the Dō Newsletter. Some of our latest and forthcoming titles include:

- *Sustainability Reporting for SMEs: Competitive Advantage Through Transparency*   Elaine Cohen
- *REDD+ and Business Sustainability: A Guide to Reversing Deforestation for Forward Thinking Companies*   Brian McFarland
- *How Gamification Can Help Your Business Engage in Sustainability*   Paula Owen
- *Sustainable Energy Options for Business*   Philip Wolfe
- *Adapting to Climate Change: 2.0 Enterprise Risk Management*   Mark Trexler & Laura Kosloff
- *How to Engage Youth to Drive Corporate Responsbility: Roles and Interventions*   Nicolò Wojewoda
- *The Short Guide to Sustainable Investing*   Cary Krosinsky
- *Strategic Sustainability: Why it Matters to Your Business and How to Make it Happen*   Alexandra McKay
- *Sustainability Decoded: How to Unlock Profit Through the Value Chain*   Laura Musikanski

- *Working Collaboratively: A Practical Guide to Achieving More*
  Penny Walker
- *Understanding G4: The Concise Guide to Next Generation Sustainability Reporting*   Elaine Cohen
- *Leading Sustainable Innovation*   Nick Coad & Paul Pritchard

Subscriptions

In addition to individual sales of our ebooks, we now offer subscriptions. Access 60+ ebooks for the price of 5 with a personal subscription to our full e-library. Institutional subscriptions are also available for your staff or students. Visit **www.dosustainability.com/books/subscriptions** or email **veruschka@dosustainability.com**

Write for us, or suggest a DōShort

Please visit **www.dosustainability.com** for our full publishing programme. If you don't find what you need, write for us! Or suggest a DōShort on our website. We look forward to hearing from you.

Abstract

NEW LEADERS ARE USING SUSTAINABILITY to help their organizations innovate and grow in response to a wide range of social, environmental, economic, and cultural issues. *Leadership for Sustainability and Change* offers a compact tune-up for professionals wanting to get the most out of their actions by providing tools to help you focus and engage in strategic action. Successful sustainability leaders use four broad sets of actions to generate personal, organizational, and social transformation, with results yielding eco-efficiency, product or service innovation, engaged communities, and market advantage. Learn from their experience how to:

- Build personal resilience to lead change for the long-run

- Identify stages of individual and organizational readiness for change

- Draw attention to what is working by focusing on the power of small differences

- Decrease resistance and increase motivation with a change acceleration model

- Use rapid prototyping to increase group engagement

- Tell compelling stories to encourage teams to initiate action

About the Authors

 **CYNTHIA SCOTT**, PhD, MPH, is an organizational change leader. As Core Faculty for the MBA, MPA, and Executive Programs at Presidio Graduate School, Cynthia provides inspiration and practical tools for leaders implementing sustainability in their organizations. She brings her 25 years of consulting experience and education in anthropology, psychology and strategic planning to Changeworks Labs, providing strategic clarity, change navigation and global leadership development. She is passionate about building organizations where engagement and innovation flourish, assisting organizations such as Walmart, WellPoint, Linked In, VmWare, Capital One, Charles Schwab, Kaiser Permanente, AT&T, Deloitte & Touche, Estee Lauder, National Semiconductor, and IBM. Cynthia is co-author of books, assessment tools, and innovative capability development programs, among them: *Agility: Fast Feedback Leadership*; *Take This Job and Love It*; *Getting Your Organization to Change*; *Empowerment*; *Rekindling Commitment*; *Navigating Change*; *Organizational Mission, Vision and Values*; *The Values Edge*; and *Self Renewal*.

 **TAMMY ESTEVES**, PhD. Tammy brings both practical and academic experience to the field of public administration, thus preferring the moniker 'pracademic'. Tammy is a tenured faculty member with Troy University, an adjunct professor with the Presidio Graduate School and has also taught courses for NC State, Virginia Commonwealth University, the University of Richmond, Christopher Newport University, and Indiana State University. She was also a guest lecturer at Bocconi University in Milan, Italy. Her practical experiences include work as training coordinator for Virginia Blood Services; Human Resources Director for International AutoSport; community services coordinator for the Jefferson Area Board for Aging; development coordinator for the Virginia Discovery Museum; and Interim Executive Director for Avalon, a shelter for women and children. Tammy is very active in the American Society for Public Administration, where she is the president for the Section on Democracy and Social Justice, and is the president for the Evergreen Chapter.

Acknowledgments

WE WISH TO THANK the following individuals for their contributions to this text: Anne Sauer, MBA Candidate at Presidio Graduate School and Developmental Editor; Casimir Fornalski, Graphic Designer.

The following people have provided generative guidance and stewardship as we worked on this book. We wish to acknowledge them for their support and ongoing efforts to keep our thinking crisp and our mission strong: Dwight Collins, Ryan Cabinte, Katharine Boshkoff, Audrey Davenport, Bob Langert, Jeff Hogue, Deborah Martin, Dr Leora Waldner, Dr Jonathan Harrington, Dr Elaine Ahumada, Dr Robert Colvin, Daniel Barre, the amazing students at Bainbridge Graduate Institute, Presidio Graduate School, and Troy University, and the team at Saatchi S, Adam Werbach, Annie Longsworth, and Andrew Bryson, for making sustainability irresistible.

Contents

CONTENTS

You (Yes, You!) Can Lead Sustainability Change

MANY BOOKS ON LEADERSHIP focus on developing certain traits, skills and competencies. However, leading sustainability-focused change requires a different approach. Sustainability leaders must be more than charismatic and inspirational to get their organizations to change. Sustainable leaders use an authentic mixture of 'inside out' and 'outside in' approaches as well as personal resilience and courage to challenge our culturally embedded ideas about what works. This book provides leaders of sustainability efforts with a guide for taking leadership action through a repeating cycle of sensing, scouting, synthesizing, and steering toward sustainable change.

Who will find this book helpful?

If you are leading change related to sustainability, this book will help you:

- Navigate the process of introducing innovative approaches.

- Reinforce your commitment to being a change agent.

- Build your skills for change leadership.

- Apply the latest brain science research toward developing engagement strategies that reduce resistance with both top-down and bottom-up approaches.

- Use stories to engage others, inspiring innovation and commitment to your ideas.

- Expand your network of professionals who are leading sustainable change.

....

FIGURE 1. Change can be top-down and/or bottom-up.

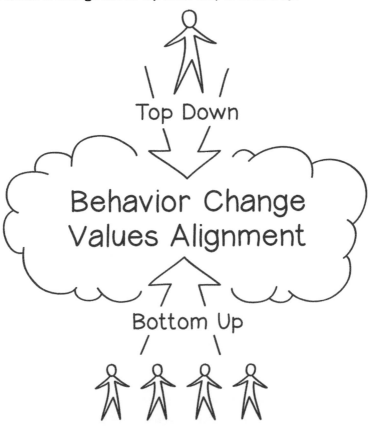

Change can come from anywhere in an organization. The change can be top-down, as when leaders or policy-makers advocate for changing policies. This occurred when McDonald's took the initiative to change the animal handling requirements with its suppliers which then strengthened the slaughterhouse behaviors in a whole industry. It can also be activated bottom-up, as when a group inside an organization changes the selection of food in the cafeteria or an external advocacy group draws attention to supply chain conditions that the organization may not be aware of.

Sustainable leaders build partnerships at both ends in order to align action and value. This dual partnership creates a check-and-balance system that keeps the focus and motivation for the change going as organizational priorities shift and provides a source of innovative ideas that keep initiatives fresh.

Audiences for this book

- **Executives** eager to use sustainability to re-position/enhance their strategy to jump ahead of the competition with something that is hard to copy: company and community culture that inspires employees by showing how their everyday work contributes to the social, economic, environmental, and cultural issues that are challenging our world.

- **Managers** ready to use sustainability to motivate employees to connect to organizational values and mission, in a time when personal connection to work matters more because benefits and incentives are decreasing.

- **Human resources managers and talent strategists** seeking to use sustainability to attract and keep the best talent and provide opportunities for engaging employees in mission-aligned activities that bridge personal and organizational purpose.

- **Brand/marketing directors** deepening their ability to use sustainability to connect customers and employees to the brand in a way that creates a compelling alignment with their personal values.

- **Corporate social responsibility/environmental health and safety professionals** expanding the focus of their efforts beyond strictly environmental issues to safety programs, brand ambassadorship, and civic engagement among their employees.

- **Organizational effectiveness professionals** leveraging sustainability to provide a focal point that connects employees to a larger shared mission and vision for their work, bringing together various organizational interests.

- **Community/government leaders** using sustainability principles to lead change in their communities, build civic capital, and enhance resilience.

- **Anyone** picking up another DōShort who is looking for the tools that will support their success in implementing that sustainability action.

....

PART 1

A New Leader is Emerging

A NEW SET OF LEADERS IS EMERGING that uses a dynamic set of skills and capabilities to recreate the economic, social, environmental, and cultural models needed to create the innovative systems, products, cultures, and operations that their organizations will need to thrive in a complex, global environment.

These sustainability leaders are emerging within operations, manufacturing, marketing, environmental health and safety, human resources, and across functions as chief sustainability officers, directors of public affairs, directors of employee engagement, mayors, city managers, civic leaders, etc. They are pioneers, many in roles that are newly formed or expanding their scope to provide strategic guidance and targeted implementation of a wide range of initiatives. These leaders are using sustainability as a 'strange attractor' to draw unlikely allies into a wave of engagement and commitment to making change that matters.

They use a broad set of engagement strategies and personal agility to face the challenges of doubt, resistance, and the complexity of getting things done across many interests. They use inner resilience and foster collaborative relationships to build long-lasting change.

We have seen sustainable leaders come to their work along two main paths: they either have the responsibility for initiating sustainability-focused work thrust upon them, or they initiate these roles as 'intrapreneurs', engaging their organizations from a values-based conviction that change in this direction is necessary. A few have the opportunity to receive targeted education in sustainable leadership from the innovative programs at Presidio Graduate School and Bainbridge Graduate School where sustainability thinking is integrated into all courses. Most have initiated their own learning path.

This book is designed to give you an intensive leadership 'tune-up' so you can integrate sustainability into strategy – whichever path you happen to be taking. We will provide Application Exercises throughout where you can stop and apply the fundamentals being taught to your own situation.

This book draws from frameworks and tools built over the last eight years in the Sustainable and Civic Leadership classes at Presidio Graduate School and Troy University. It features Case Stories that highlight the experiences of the 750 graduates of these Sustainable Leadership programs who are designing and implementing innovative sustainable change out in the world alongside the stories of numerous pioneers of sustainability initiatives, all of whom we have had the privilege to work with, who are pushing ahead even though they don't have all the answers.

Sustainability is a journey

It is common for sustainability leaders to hold a clear a vision of where they would like to be and at the same time understand the current state of their organization's practices. This gap creates a dynamic tension for action.

Too big of a gap can also prevent action as people sometimes feel that they have too far to go, resulting in avoidance. A change leader acts as a

FIGURE 2. Leaders hold tension between the current state and a vision for the future.

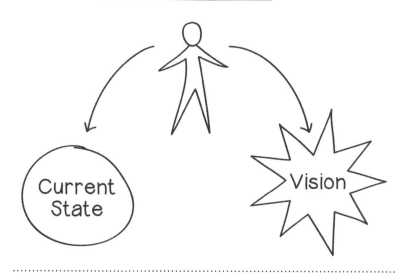

bridge, holding this tension by creating a path so that people can catch the vision and have the courage to begin.

People and organizations can become depleted if they see too big a gap between where they are and where they want to be. A change leader can reduce this gap by asking where the organization is currently sustainable and identifying what is already working. Instead of focusing on problems, focus on the possibilities. This energizes people to see that there is already forward movement to build upon.

Leading sustainability efforts is never smooth, and because innovation is a series of iterative steps, you will predictably stumble a few times. It is important to keep 'falling' in the direction that you want to go, seeing each successive effort as part of a larger strategic focus. All leaders have had this experience, even if they do not readily talk about it. The most important factor is how you reset your focus and renew your momentum. Acknowledging, learning, and trying again are key actions in leading change in organizations.

New leaders need new skills

At the core of sustainable leadership is the ability to be an agile leader and facilitator of change. Agility requires advanced capabilities in strategy formation and execution in complex, multi-stakeholder environments. The systemic nature of many of these changes calls on sophisticated approaches to leading organizations and the people in them.

You must be able to navigate individual, group, and whole organizational systems to translate ideas and technical expertise into desired actions. Change leadership requires both strategic vision and day-to-day conversations as well as actions that call for a level of personal resilience and agility that can challenge the most seasoned leader.

This book was written to help you develop those capabilities and lead your organization to the change you envision.

PART 2

Navigational Tools For Leaders

THE PATH TO SUSTAINABILITY CAN BE LONG, full of obstacles and opportunities for missteps, and is often uncharted. In this section, we will provide you with the frameworks and tools successful sustainability leaders use to guide their organizations toward powerful visions for the future.

Beware of benchmarking

There is no one magic path to success. Other organizations' experiences can provide inspiration and guidance, but in our experience each successful implementation is the result of many choices based on a unique set of conditions.

Leaders use a combination of approaches to create and steer the sustainability initiatives in their organizations. It can be tempting to look for best practices and apply them to your situation because they have led to success elsewhere. However, each organization has its own history, culture and special challenges, and what works for one organization will not necessarily work for another. Sustainability change is most successful when engagement and involvement is catalyzed throughout the organization.

Because of the broad systemic nature of sustainability-focused challenges, it is necessary to go slow to go fast: be willing to take more time to customize and identify unique leverage points in the beginning. We have seen a set of four actions that have framed the approaches of a number of sustainability leaders.

Sense, scout, synthesize, steer

Sustainability leaders take four repeatable navigational actions to create strategy and engage employees and communities to make change and move towards a thriving future. These actions are repeated over and over

....

FIGURE 3. Sustainability leaders need to sense, scout, synthesize, and steer.

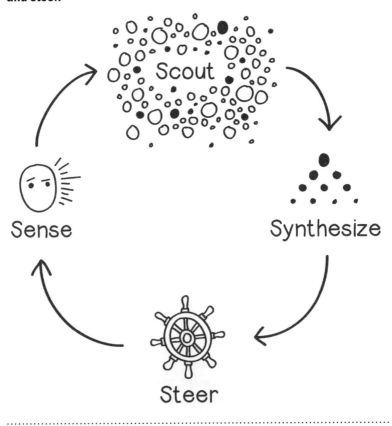

in the process of designing and implementing change. They can provide a framework for focusing and sequencing your leadership approach, over the course of multiple initiatives. By taking these actions, you will produce fresh engagement and focus, enabling follow-through and implementation to take place.

1. **Sense:** Identify your purpose. Connect your core values to your personal intention to become resilient and establish a foundation for leading change.

2. **Scout:** Look around you. Understand and appreciate the stages of transition, assess organizational and individual readiness, and identify key people and leverage points for change.

3. **Synthesize:** Find patterns and build commitment. Map your change journey, design, test, and evolve approaches with rapid feedback, and engage others with stories of progress.

4. **Steer:** Implement and calibrate. Mobilize action, track progress, encourage feedback, and continue to grow.

These actions are supported by tools and frameworks that are not specific to sustainability. They represent the approach of leaders who use their personal values to engage others in developing and implementing changes that improve performance and increase innovation. These leadership skills are not new but have been gaining validity as an alternative to more traditional tell-and-sell leadership. The most successful leaders in sustainability are using these positive, collaborative approaches to engage all levels of their organizations in continuous change.

FIGURE 3a. These actions are repeated over and over in the process of designing and implementing change.

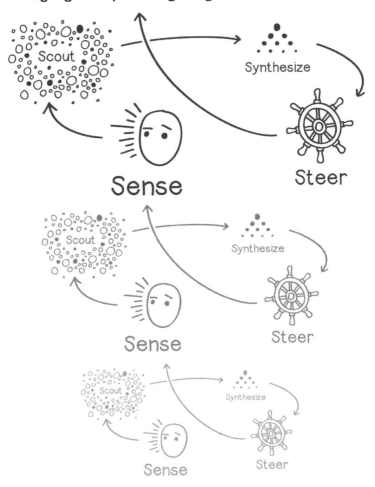

Sense: Identify your purpose

Welcome to the world of being a change agent. Whether or not you have chosen this role for yourself, change leadership has chosen you. This is an invitation to lean into change, to take initiative for advocating and activating multiple energies to create change. Creating change in your organization means starting with yourself. An organization can only go as far as its leaders: you will only ever be able to create as much change as you can tolerate yourself. It is important to know who you are and why you're doing what you're doing. Understanding these things will provide a foundation for you to create lasting change.

Leading sustainability change requires both short-term action and long-term perseverance. There are two clear areas where successful sustainability leaders seem to excel. First, they have the ability to structure and facilitate collaborative engagement with a number of stakeholders. Second, they have the ability to stay the course as both organizational and cultural values shift.

CASE STORY

Bob Langert, VP of Corporate Social Responsibility at McDonald's has been with the company for over 30 years. He started out working in logistics and ended up in sustainability leadership by accident. In 1998, he was assigned to a temporary position working on environmental initiatives like phasing out the use of CFCs in McDonald's packaging. While in this position, he had the epiphany that this was what he loved to do: blending business with making a positive impact on the world. When the first VP

---

of environmental affairs stepped down, Bob asked the general council if he could take over. Making this request took him out of his comfort zone, but he was motivated to make this kind of work a bigger part of his life. Since then, Bob has led McDonald's to form a partnership with the Environmental Defense Fund, create worldwide animal welfare standards with the assistance of Dr Temple Grandin, and work with Greenpeace to place a moratorium on ingredients coming from rainforest land, among other things. He leads values work at McDonald's not by proscribing how to live values but by share stories about how people are living their values to make a difference.

Build personal resilience

It takes stamina to keep holding the tension between your vision for the future and the current state of the organization. Leaders of sustainability initiatives are change agents, and change agents get burned out because they care. Thankfully, you can develop the hardiness and resilience to stay the course. Here are four personal practices that people who thrive through this kind of large-scale change use as a foundation for their personal resilience, ensuring that they have the stamina for life-long contribution:

- **Coherence:** Connect your work to your personal and professional values and passions. Create a personal story of 'why' you are doing what you are doing. Remind yourself of your story and tell it to others, and help other people come to their own understanding of why they are engaged in their work.

- **Control:** Act where you are. Focus on things that you can influence and let go of what you can't. Start small, with your own everyday actions, habits, and choices, and let this change be a spark that ignites action in other people, building forward momentum.

- **Challenge:** Take on things outside of your comfort zone. Identify an area that will enhance one of your strengths. Encourage yourself to find ways to go beyond your current thinking about what is possible. Be curious about what people are doing in other organizations.

- **Connection:** Seek out other change agents and learn from their perspectives. Loners do not create much change. People change most directly from being in relationships, not from watching power points or reading memos, and your ability to emotionally connect to others will increase your ability to change. Let people know what you are doing – reach out and get encouragement from peers, and provide support to colleagues.

Application Exercise: Identify your core intention

Instead of leaving your values at the door, bring them into your work environment. Establishing a personal connection to sustainability can provide an authentic foundation for taking organizational action and creates a strong leverage point for change. Use your personal passion to identify opportunities for organizational action.

What are you passionate about?

_____

_____

Where does your passion come from?

_____

_____

What opportunities do you see for change, i.e. efficiency and brand leadership?

_____

_____

What personal experiences have led you to care about making changes that support more sustainable ways of doing business?

_____

_____

Sustainability change gains momentum

When it comes to change leadership, always remember that you are in good company. Attention to sustainability has risen dramatically in the last five years, and Accenture has been tracing the attitudes and approaches towards sustainability. Its 2011 study found that 67% of C-suite decision-makers in the United States, the United Kingdom, and China said that sustainability is very important to their company, and 72% thought the benefits of their sustainability initiatives exceeded expectations, especially around brand attributes, like improved reputation and consumer trust, and costs.

The largest barriers to driving sustainability initiatives are lack of interest and belief in benefits. These are the areas where leadership can have the most effect. Recently, a number of key thought leaders have affirmed that sustainability will be an area that leaders will need to incorporate into their strategic and operational thinking, including Santiago Gowland, formerly with Unilever and currently GM for Sustainable Business & Innovation at NIKE, who said: 'The only way to continue growing and continue being a successful business is to treat sustainability as a key business lever in the same way that you treat marketing, finance, culture, HR or supply chain.'

Sustainability as an action hub

Because sustainability represents environmental, economic, cultural, and social elements of impact, it is a big tent for gathering seemingly disconnected programs, initiatives, and efforts. For example, health and wellness promotion efforts can be seen as an extension of personal sustainability practices, a community project that supports physical exercise as well as civic engagement.

Become curious and explore opportunity

Sustainability can provide a refreshed perspective, helping you connect focused efforts to larger organizational initiatives. As you begin to look for the connections between your organizations' products, services, and strategy, you will identify relationships that may have not been fully optimized. Think beyond your usual focus and begin to see what unintended consequences emerge from the impact of your organization.

Scout: Look around you

Before rushing ahead toward your vision for the future, you need to understand how human beings respond to change and where the people in your organization are in that process. Different stages of adoption require different approaches, and using the wrong approach will result in fleeting changes rather than lasting results. This section provides you with a few different frameworks for observing and understanding what is going on around you so that you can develop appropriate strategies for achieving your goal.

Starting where you are

First, take some time to identify where your organization currently stands when it comes to sustainability. Opportunities for sustainability often manifest in multiple areas of an organization. Setting a strategy for sustainability efforts or connecting them to already existing strategic initiatives provides firm footing for building shared commitment and momentum.

Thinking about progress toward sustainability as a continuum provides a way to consolidate multiple perspectives and experiences into a continuous process. Using the following model in our consulting practice at Saatchi & Saatchi S, helped us help clients adjust their expectations and match the approach to the organizational readiness.

Each phase represents specific opportunities for sustainability activation:

- **Not aware:** Introducing education about what others are doing. This could mean attending conferences or circulating examples of reports that demonstrate the strategic importance of sustainability.

- **Waking up:** Connecting small actions to larger existing initiatives. Lean manufacturing efforts connect to sustainability in this stage.

- **Compliance:** Responding to regulations so as to keep up with industry standards. Up-to-date practices are encouraged.

FIGURE 4. Phases of sustainability adoption.

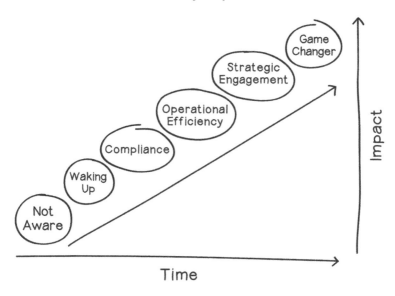

- **Operational efficiency:** Targeting cost savings related to performance, efficiency, and waste. Blends with other process improvement and safety efforts.

- **Strategic engagement:** Connecting efforts to brand positioning. This could mean engaging employees and customers to take action on behalf of values based issues.

- **Game changer:** Making bold promises and following through on them, like committing to making the organization zero waste, or using industry visibility for leadership of innovative approaches.

Don't fall into the trap of trying to implement actions that are out of sync with your organizations' current phase – for example, wanting to launch a brand communication campaign (strategic engagement) before basic health and safety practices (compliance) are in place. An appetite for fast change has landed numerous organizations in the 'greenwashing' camp, talking the talk without walking the walk. To avoid this disconnect, keep your efforts aligned with the phase(s) in which your organization can demonstrate effective efforts. Recognize the phase in which your organization is currently functioning, and use it to guide the development of your strategy as you learn about the rest of the frameworks.

Thinking in systems

Sustainability leaders need know how to see the larger systems in which they live and work so that they can go beyond superficial fixes to offer strategic ways of addressing challenges that to many seem outside of their control. They must be able to step back and develop a broad understanding of the whole system that they are working in. Sustainability leaders need to gather data across a wide range of sources, quickly explore what others have done, talk to people who are touched by sustainability efforts, and learn from people who are not aware of the impact they could have.

To do this, leaders must think and engage their organizations in multiple ways by observing what is happening at four different levels, as identified by Peter Senge in *The Necessary Revolution*:

LEVEL	DESCRIPTION	SUSTAINABILITY EXAMPLES
1. Events	One time actions that draw immediate attention to sustainability issues	• Product recall • Beach clean up • Reusable cup month
2. Patterns	Look for repeat occurrences of issues and topics	• Cluster of customer complaints across industry • More attendance at events themed toward sustainability
3. Trends	The deeper forces and structures that contribute to these patterns	• Increased awareness of interest in product ingredients and manufacturing sources • Emphasis on engaging in shared efforts toward common goals
4. Core beliefs and assumptions	The thinking patterns and assumptions that have allowed these trends to develop	• Safe products increase profitability • Local action matters

Because sustainability manifests across multiple levels in an organization, it must be understood in a larger context in order to identify all leverage points for change. All these levels are important for leading change in an organization. Change can begin in the form of an initiative or event that draws attention to broader patterns and trends. Examining the underlying assumptions and beliefs that create the pattern of actions can help identify larger shifts in strategy.

Application Exercise: Levels of sustainability in your organization

Identifying examples in your own organization may lead to the discovery of other levels of change, awareness of additional leverage points for accomplishing your goals, as well as new opportunities for improvement. Using the explanations above, identify opportunities in your organization.

LEVEL	EXAMPLES IN YOUR ORGANIZATION
1. Events	
2. Patterns	
3. Trends	
4. Core beliefs and assumptions	

Focus on what's working

In all organizations there are people who are succeeding despite the inadequacy of the processes and structures that are in place. Their actions are often ignored or undervalued because the results they produce, though positive, are neither highly visible nor measurable. This concept of 'positive deviance' came out of social science research that began to look for and focus on people whose results did not fit the standard, inquiring into what they were they doing that made the difference.

Applying this thinking to sustainable leadership, it is important to search for and notice the small things that people are already doing to create positive change. This goes against the tradition of celebrating heroic efforts while often ignoring the smaller everyday actions that contribute to cumulative gains. When leaders pay attention to these smaller efforts, they encourage other people to make similar efforts, generating more energy and causing results to build. What the leader notices can gain attention and often what started as a small action will have a large ripple effect.

CASE STORY

An associate who had been volunteering as a Personal Sustainability Practice (PSP) Captain at Walmart, took a look around as he had been trained to do, seeking small things that could make a difference in energy, waste, and personal behavior. What he noticed was that the solar panel that they carried in the automotive department could be adapted to work on the 'cart pushers' in the parking lot. The store managers' team investigated and decided with the guidance of leadership and management team that it would work perfectly. They installed solar panels on their cart pushers and the entire team communicated the results with other teams and their families. The idea was recognized and highlighted in a positive local newspaper article. They also tracked the energy usage for the corporate sustainability team, who estimated that the idea would save $200 in energy costs per cart pusher per year. When you multiply that by the number of cart pushers per store, and the number of stores across the nation, the potential impact on preserving our natural resources is huge.

CASE STORY

A similar initiative, which encouraged small steps and innovative ideas in sustainability at Saatchi & Saatchi branch offices worldwide, netted this list of personal sustainability practices generated by the employees at the Shanghai office:

- Keep recycled bags with you

- Stop throwing away chopsticks

- Develop the habit of turning off the light

- Draw smaller when you are doing a layout

- Use electronic editions for making internal reviews

Because the ideas were generated by employees themselves, they had a much greater chance of being adopted and leading to sustained behavior change than people being 'voluntold' to take up top-down practices. There is always a tension between implementing sweeping change and leaving room for individuals to add their own innovation and initiative, and that tension is worth holding.

Holding tension

Sustainability leaders need to have the ability to function in two realities: holding the aspiration of a more sustainable future while at the same time focusing on current state actions. These realities represent two versions of the truth and often require maintaining a focus on and respect for the existing system while building the new one. Very often, a current way of doing and thinking is coming to an end due to increased awareness, new initiatives, or shifts in other systems. These patterns are deeply embedded and provide value in the environment in which they were constructed, even if they may not continue to provide value to the new reality that is being built.

The S curve below models how two competing realities can exist at the same time. Sustainability leaders must create the broad shift represented by the second curve, while at the same time acknowledging the efforts that brought the organization to its current level of performance represented by the first curve. In this way, these curves show the tension that the organization is experiencing.

FIGURE 5. The hashing in this S curve illustrates the tension between the current level of performance and the future goal.

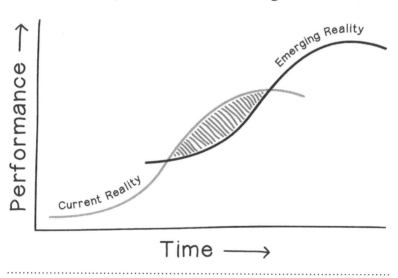

CASE STORY

Jim Rogers, former CEO of Duke Energy, advocated during his tenure at the company for investing in energy efficiency, modernizing the electric infrastructure, and pursuing advanced technologies and nuclear energy to grow the economy and transition to a low-carbon future. He serves as Vice Chairman of the World Business Council for Sustainable Development. Declaring that there could be a low carbon future for one of the largest coal-burning energy companies is a perfect example of a leader managing the tension of the S curve.

Application Exercise: Where do you hold tension?

Identify the current reality and emerging reality in your organization between which you hold the tension.

....

FIGURE 5a. Label your own S curve on the dotted lines.

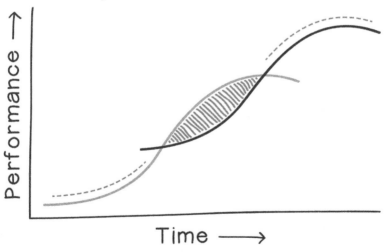

....

Accelerating adoption

Leading sustainability-related change requires a keen understanding of where to put your effort and attention. One of the challenges you face is that the future is already here; it is just not distributed equally. Some people in your organization are still focused on the current reality, while others have already moved on to the future. How do you engage both of these groups to keep the organization going forward?

In *Diffusion of Innovations*, Everett M. Rogers provided a simple way of thinking about how to approach behavior change: he determined that people's responses to change fall along a continuum, ranging from actively resisting change to actively innovating. The following curve is a snapshot of a point in time during a period of organizational change illustrating that different people react to change in different ways:

- **No commitment**
    - Passive or active resistance
    - Denying reality
    - Tend to impede the progress of the entire group

- **Let it happen**
    - Laissez-faire attitude
    - Observers
    - Believe the change will go away eventually

- **Help it happen**
    - Lend a hand where necessary
    - Participants
    - Support the change, but do not provide substantial leadership

FIGURE 6. A snapshot of how different people in an organization are reacting to change at a given point in time.

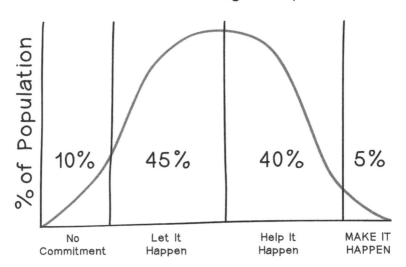

Distribution of Change Adoption

Openness to Change

- Make it happen
  - Drive the change process
  - Leaders
  - Demonstrate a high level of commitment and foster the commitment of others

At any point in time, the number of people in each category of reaction may be greater or fewer, moving toward commitment as time progresses, but there will always be a distribution and you will never get everybody out of the first category.

Application Exercise: Take a snapshot

Estimate what percentage of people in your organization or group is in each category and draw a curve to match. This will help you when you need to approach people in different stages of adoption.

....

FIGURE 6a. Label the buckets and draw a curve illustrating the percentage of people in your organization that fall into each category.

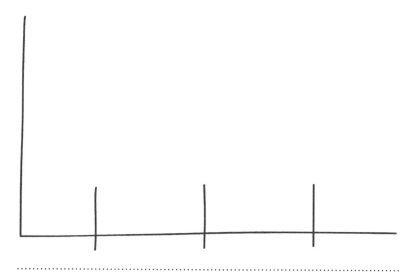

....

Navigating the human side of change

How can understanding why some people take a longer time to adapt to change help sustainability leaders accelerate change within their organizations? By using this understanding of the human side of behavior change to develop leadership strategies for engaging and reducing the cycle time of change, leaders can manage through the predictable stages of change adaptation.

Improving change adaptability

Assessing where the individuals, teams, and whole systems you work with are in relation to the change you are promoting can help you respond in ways that accelerate adaptation.

Application Exercise: Change leaders go first

To be a good leader of change, it is important to understand your own pattern of response, so you can use this as a foundation for understanding others. While your response pattern will not be the same as that of other people, you will gain an appreciation for the experience of the emotional path through change.

To begin, identify a significant change that you have experienced in your life. This can be something from your past or something you are experiencing right now. Choose a change that required you to shift your basic patterns of behavior, like a job change, health challenge, or other major life transition (marriage, children being born or leaving home, divorce, etc.).

My significant change

Recall your thoughts, feelings, and actions...

...before the change happened

...when it was happening

...when it was more than half-way accomplished

...and at the end

Did you initiate the change, or did the change happen to you?

These questions identify a predictable path that people experience as they adapt to change. They correspond to the four phases of the Transition Curve, first discussed in *Rekindling Commitment* by Jaffe and Scott, which provides a model for understanding how individuals and organizations respond to change.

The Transition Curve

There are four predictable phases that people go through to embrace change:

- **Denying:** Putting off change. People may demonstrate denying by 'missing' the meeting or email, not learning the new technology, etc. Alternatively, they may respond by doing more of the old way faster, harder, more emphatically, resulting in high performance but in a way that only supports the former strategy.

- **Resisting:** Emotional disruption (complaining, blaming, upset, anger, sadness, etc.) is a result of breaking basic patterns of behavior or belief. This is normal for people who are faced with large changes that disrupt very basic certainty, such as resetting of values and beliefs about consumption (more is better), natural resource use (there is always more), right to operate (ownership = control).

FIGURE 7. When faced with change, people go through denying, resisting, exploring, and committing as time passes, moving from external concerns to internal and back to external.

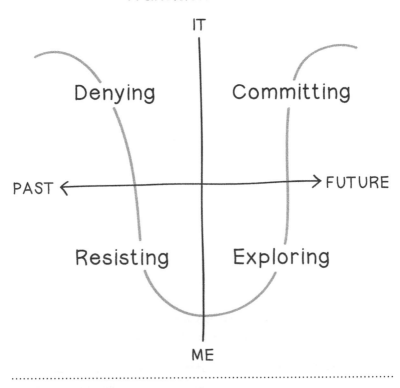

- **Exploring**: Renewed interest, innovative ideas, and finding applications are actions that represent a return to thinking about the future and having the energy to seek out and try options. People have enthusiasm for new ideas, which can lead to an overflow of ideas and unfocused action. This is a time of potential chaos and it requires focus and guidance from leadership.

- **Committing**: Establishing new patterns and methods. This phase signals the end of disruption and a return to a pattern of behavior and actions that support performance and learning. People can get things done, pay attention to customer needs, and focus their attention on thinking about the next innovation.

How the change is initiated makes a difference

When people are faced with a change, they start from one of two different points: having initiated the change or having the change initiated from somewhere else. This difference in volition has a big impact on how they move through the change.

People who initiate the change often do so as a result of frustration with the way things are or realization that the current state cannot be maintained. People who are 'changed' as the result of other's decisions or circumstances outside their control can experience an extended time of denying that the change is happening to maintain a sense of control. This denial or even a lack of awareness that the change is happening is connected to our uniquely human capability of not paying attention to things that are threatening or overwhelming. In the case of sustainability, this response may arise due to the large scale of the challenges sustainability efforts attempt to address (natural resource scarcity, climate change, agricultural changes, etc.). People are well-equipped with the ability to not notice things that provoke such great threat.

People who initiate change under their own volition still go through denial, as we all have an innate bias toward not changing comfortable, familiar patterns, even if the change represents an improvement (for example, moving into a new house that you wanted still means experiencing the disruption of having to re-arrange all your belongings and create new patterns).

Which of these paths an individual takes is often determined by the level of control that the individual feels over the changes taking place. When the change is initiated by factors outside of your direct control, it is normal to use denial to reduce the threat. As people find ways to exert even small amounts of control, however, or if they themselves initiated the change, they are able to take a more empowered stance in the face of change.

Leading change

There is no specific amount of time needed for each phase of the Transition Curve. In the case of a small change, like switching to double-sided copying, people can experience all four of these phases – denying, resisting, exploring, committing – in the course of a one-hour meeting. On the other hand, changes that require larger shifts in core beliefs, like switching your whole supplier network due to a new emphasis on human rights, usually require longer adjustment time, as they challenge people's sense of certainty, status, and fairness.

It is crucial for leaders to identify and understand the behaviors associated with each of these phases and to use approaches that can accelerate the individual, team, or organization to move more quickly from denying and resisting toward taking committed action.

Leading through each phase

Leaders of sustainability changes do best when they apply different strategies and behaviors to each stage. Be careful to use leadership strategies that match the emotional stage of the employees you're

FIGURE 8. Leaders should engage each stage of the Transition Curve with actions designed to help people continue forward: Wake up, listen, focus, acknowledge.

addressing. An inspirational talk about the future to people who are successfully denying that there is a need for change will fall on deaf ears. On the flip side, making an argument about why sustainability innovation is important to people who are ready to take action will lead to frustration and high performing talent to question their commitment. Sustainability leaders must understand how to shift their attention when a critical mass of people shifts from one phase to another.

It is important to help people move through the phases in order – jumping ahead, from denying to committing, results in the leader thinking that change has been accomplished when in fact people are still resisting and not ready to move forward.

DENYING

A leader's role during the denying phase is to provide data and personalized experiences of the new reality to help people make the connection to why the change is necessary. Hearing directly from customers, reviewing trend data about what other organizations in your industry are doing, discussing market analyses, seeing the impact of not changing, etc., can provide a shared context for people to understand the need for change.

CASE STORY

Working with a small-town newspaper that needed to expand its audience to survive being faced with a largely non-English-speaking/reading population in their service area, the leader arranged for field trips to the communities to meet and understand these new customers. When they found that Spanish radio was

---

the way they sought their news and commerce, the newspaper reporters, sales staff and managers realized that their former approach was not going to be viable in the future.

Leaders can follow this kind of wake-up call by providing data and direct experiences that draw connections to their visions for the future. It is common for people and organizations deep in denying to not hear several rounds of wake-up calls. With sustainability, it is often an external watchdog organization that finally draws the attention to the issue (child labor, toxics, rainforest sourcing, etc.).

RESISTING

Resisting is a very important phase as it allows people to experience the loss of comfort, pattern, and certainty that is part of any substantial change. Changes related to sustainability threaten core beliefs about success, satisfaction, and enterprise viability that have been built up across generations and are embedded in our community and work cultures. Because the related thought and behavior patterns have been practiced over and over, they are deeply engrained in our brains, and disturbing these patterns can set off reactions that are unconscious and hard to control. You cannot fix people's discomfort; you can only help them identify it and express it so they can move themselves forward. Rushing them through this will only encourage people to pretend to commit and will undermine trust and performance. Leaders who can invite and listen to and acknowledge the experience of disruption tend to assist their organizations in moving forward more smoothly, in less time.

CASE STORY

When Walmart engaged its employees to learn about sustainability actions they used a peer-to-peer, relationship-building approach. They asked for volunteers to be trained as store captains to go back and encourage their peers to take up personal sustainability practices (PSPs). They buffered the challenging messages about climate change and resource scarcity by using trusted, specially trained peers to engage others in action.

Remember that misapplying the listening strategy for resisting to an organization/group that is actually in the denying stage tends to provide the leader with a false sense of commitment. Encouraging people to express their reactions to the disruption in town hall meetings, online forums, etc. jump starts the movement from denying to resisting. This expression of resisting is a positive step because it means that people are noticing something is happening, and that it is going to affect them.

EXPLORING AND COMMITTING

When employees begin to have ideas and interest in taking up new actions they need leadership to help them focus. It is a good time for skill development and training. Acknowledging those who are making contributions and innovation helps encourage others to move forward.

Going beyond blame and shame

Many approaches to change have been shaped by the identification of a gap between where you are and some external benchmark. Identifying this gap and then closing it consumes a lot of energy and effort, which often results in an atmosphere of competitive blame-and-shame holding up others' efforts in the hopes of creating change. Once thought to provide motivation, we now know that this approach actually has the opposite effect, making people feel less capable of change. Especially with sustainability issues (climate change, resource scarcity, technological limits, etc.), the gaps are often so large as to have the potential to create a sense of overwhelming inertia, as people feel like nothing they do will make enough change to cause a difference fast enough, if at all.

Effective leaders do not abandon thinking about gaps but often use an additional approach of focusing on what is working to harness an untapped source of energy for mobilizing effort. People's brains react differently when they are asked to focus on what makes them happy, what is working, or what they appreciate. This appreciative inquiry approach, described by Diana Whitney and Amanda Trosten-Bloom in *The Power of Appreciative Inquiry*, has become a strong force for shaping the entry points for change. If you begin with what people are proud of and what they cherish, they can use that energy to engage with change.

CASE STORY

The Personal Sustainability Champions at Walmart began their training by being asked to identify and say out loud what makes them happy. People identified playing with children, pets, families, parks, and being in nature. As part of their personal sustainability practice (PSP) they were then challenged to identify one small behavior that could help them support that happiness. People chose to stop using one-use bottles, reduce the amount of beef eaten and canned beverages they consumed, and to cook at home and exercise more. These 'Nano Practices' gave them a sense of confidence that they

---

could then apply to other changes. It also created a foundation for having a happiness-based conversation with others, which aided them in getting others to join them in their efforts.

EXPLORING

The exploring phase is a time when people are done grieving the loss of pattern and begin to focus on what can be done with the new idea. They have high energy and lots of ideas for potential action. Leaders in this phase need to empower a range of actions. This is a time for exploring ideas, starting pilots, rapid prototyping, innovation teams, and short-term experiments to see what approaches provide the most impact. Do not be concerned about the potential chaos caused by going multiple directions in this phase. Allow ideas and launch pilot projects and quick-turn iterations to see what catches interest and supports the new direction. Provide focus on a couple of areas and let people be creative within those areas. Be prepared for surprises and listen to people who have out-of-the-box ideas.

COMMITTING

Committing signals the end of the transition and a return to a pattern of behavior and actions that support performance and learning. This is a time to consolidate and refine new policies, to affirm values and direction. It is important for the leader to recognize the contributions of everyone for having let go of the old and embracing the new direction. Use celebrations to acknowledge how far the change has brought the organization and begin to mobilize energy for potential changes in the future.

CASE STORY

The following is an example of a leader who successfully moved his group through the creative chaos of exploring to the focus of committing. A multi-office law firm launched a sustainable action initiative, empowering local offices to do whatever they wanted to promote sustainability. The resulting barrage of activities and ideas turned out to be a work distraction, with competitions springing up between offices, culminating in a YouTube video contest: an inter-office rap battle about they were doing to be sustainable. The senior partner who introduced the initiative acknowledged the internal competition by declaring a winner and publishing their video on their internal site, and then helped refocus this energy on external community activation that could be branded across all offices. The firm used this community activation as an example of employee engagement that won them a place on the '100 Best Companies to Work For' list sponsored by Fortune and the Best Places to Work Institute.

The Transition Curve model helps you match your leadership behaviors to specific stages to enhance performance. Leaders use different approaches based on which stage of change the individuals and teams they work with are in. People do not move straight ahead through the Transition Curve; they often move back and forth between stages, depending on how challenging the change is. It is possible for people to move more quickly through change if they have built up a set of practices from previous changes, thoughts and actions that tend to increase resilience and agility. We will identify and describe them later in this book.

Application Exercise: Identifying signs of change

Think about the individuals in your organization that are affected by the change you are pursuing. What specific behaviors have you noticed from people in each of the four stages? How have you addressed these behaviors, and how do you plan to do so going forward?

PHASE	INDIVIDUAL BEHAVIOR	LEADERSHIP ACTION	WHAT YOU NOTICE	ACTIONS YOU HAVE TAKEN/ PLAN TO TAKE
Denying	Business as usual, extra effort put into old behaviors	Wake up to new reality, field trip to new environment, provide data, hands-on observation		
Resisting	Upset with change, non-productive, angry, overwhelmed	Identify the loss, understand the disruption, listen to distress		
Exploring	Actively trying many solutions, enjoying new ideas	Provide focus for action, help eliminate unproductive behaviors		
Committing	New routines and behaviors in place	Celebration of impact, acknowledge progress		

Synthesize: Finding patterns and building commitment

With a clear understanding of where different people in your organization are when it comes to accepting the coming changes and how to vary your approach to meet them where they are, you can now pull together your approach and engage people in your plans. As you do, be sure to acknowledge what came before, and elicit the collaboration of those around you in making the journey – the more ownership people feel over the vision they're striving towards, the more likely the change is to stick.

Map the change journey

The best sustainability leaders we have seen do two things simultaneously: they engage a broad conversation to create a shared vision of a compelling future, and they identify a path to reach that goal, creating aspirational tension that can guide action. This can be done by creating a 'map' of the current environment that the organization is navigating. A map can be a communication tool for conveying the big picture idea of what you are trying to accomplish. In addition to illustrating the destination and desired outcome, it identifies the history of your organization that has brought you to the point of taking this next step, as well as significant trends and business challenges that are making it vital to pay attention to the sustainability issues at hand and partnerships needed to reach the goal. Establishing a powerful vision and then showing the navigation path for moving through the stages of strategic action provides leadership for change.

Setting up this idea of a journey rather than a diagnosis gives people in the organization a way to see change as an ongoing process, rather than something that is 'managed' once and gotten over with. Maps, from ancient parchments to modern GPS units, are universally understood as a metaphor for tools that help people know where they are, steer around barriers, and find their destinations safely. Because all maps are imperfect and cannot show the up-to-the-moment changes in the environment (like traffic jams or disruptive competitors) they support the discovery and incorporation of new information to update the route. The map will be most effective if a broad group of people is involved in its creation. The more people contribute to building the future, the more they will own it and support it.

It can be tempting for leaders to want to skip over talking about historic choices and actions and just focus on the current state and the path forward. However, having people talk about their organization's history provides an opportunity to acknowledge past learnings and accomplishments by reminding people of their resilience and adaptability. Looking backward to go forward builds enduring momentum and courage for change.

Change journey maps

A change journey map shows how the organization's history and current actions are connected to sustainability. These maps provide a coherent picture of how actions from the past are connected to a desired future vision. Leaders use these maps to explain why change is necessary and to acknowledge past efforts and frame current choices.

A change journey map includes the elements that good maps have always had:

- **History:** founding vision, significant leaders, milestones, challenges
- **Current state:** where are we now

FIGURE 9. Change journey map.

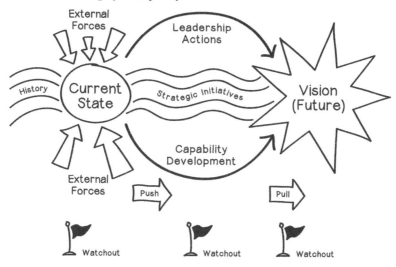

- **External forces:** what trends, market conditions, customer requirements, regulations are bringing this focus on sustainability

- **Future vision:** where do we want to be, what will a thriving future hold?

- **Strategic initiatives:** steps to move forward, key milestones of progress, major initiatives

- **Leadership:** key actions/competencies that leaders need to use to steward the change

- **Capability development:** employee skills and mindsets, organizational policies that need to be built to support the new way

FIGURE 10. A map created to illustrate the merger of two groups to create a new enterprise.

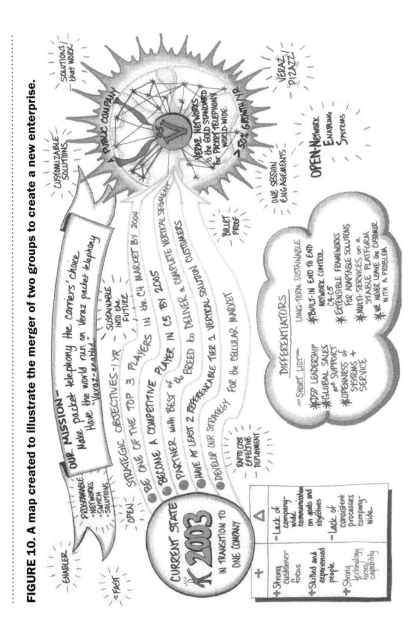

- **Watch-outs:** dangers to be avoided, potential places that the change could be derailed

Displaying all these elements on one page allows people to take a broad, systemic view of the change, rather than starting with specific functional efforts. Seeing the big picture provides guidance for taking up changes that will require sustained effort over time, which is important because many sustainability initiatives go beyond short-term fixes and require the effort of multiple groups.

A change journey map allows multiple groups to see how their collective efforts support the change and can be useful to start a conversation about what they can do to help reach the future vision. As sustainability changes move from tactical compliance- or efficiency-based interventions into supporting strategic brand and industry positioning, the need for these longer-term pictures of action becomes the foundation for telling the stories that support sustained commitment, even across future changes in leadership.

Application Exercise: Mapping your change journey

Create a map of your organization's journey toward sustainability. Identify the elements of the change journey from the list above and represent them visually in a one-page format.

High-engagement design team

The ability to create a path forward while working with imperfect data is one of the biggest challenges for sustainability leaders. Leaders may want to keep their thinking to themselves so as not to expose themselves to scrutiny from others in their organizations. However, this tactic often backfires when plans into which they have put a lot of work do not get implemented, resulting in wasted effort and decreasing trust in leadership. As organizations experience repeated waves of promises and failed implementation, they often adopt a survivor mentality – keep your head down, pull back, and just focus on your work.

We recommend that leaders to set up a cross-functional design team, consisting of people representing employees and community members impacted by the change, that can digest the data and examine the patterns of action that have formed in order to create a plan for implementation. This step is often missed because of the effort required to organize multiple sources of input or the fear that it will take too long or never become focused. However, while it is messy to sort through lots of opinions and ideas, avoiding this step can lead to one of the biggest mistakes leaders can make: spending too much time planning with a small group of 'strategic' thinkers and then rolling out the change to the group that is to take action. According to John Kotter, author of *Leading Change*, a stunning 75% large-scale changes fail, and creating a guiding coalition is a key element in creating change successfully.

Broad engagement of multiple stakeholder groups early on provides shared context that helps reduce the amount of time spent in the denying and resisting phases and increase your chances of success. Leaders should engage representative groups of people to synthesize and digest the options and launch pilots in rapid succession, to gather feedback and make quick course corrections. This emphasis on 'rapid prototyping' increases the opportunities for innovation and engagement. People will support what they help to build. It also opens the design process to more people, increasing the opportunity to identify unintended consequences of the approach and potential elements that have been neglected, creating a smoother path to implementation.

> **CASE STORY**
>
> Instead of a presenting employees with a 'voluntold' volunteer opportunity, a company decided to see what would happen if employees were asked to identify areas of interest and then vote to allocate time and resources toward completing a chosen initiative. The employees ended up instituting Reusable Cup Month where they could count their progress and waste impact.

We have seen a number of leaders using these sorts of large-scale rapid strategic planning sessions to bring people together to tackle seemingly impossible challenges:

> **CASE STORY**
>
> In *Visual Leadership*, David Sibbet describes and illustrates the process used to convert the Presidio Army base to the Golden Gate National Recreation Area. Starting in 1989, the Presidio planning team worked for six years getting citizen input with six large visioning meetings. To facilitate this process they created a large roadmap that showed six stages: 1) initiation and research; 2) visioning and analysis; 3) alternatives development; 4) drafting the plan; 5) final plan preparation; and 6) implementation.

> **CASE STORY**
>
> As his city tried to recover from bankruptcy, Osby Davis, Mayor of Vallejo, California, worked with the City Council to develop the nation's first Citywide Participatory Budgeting process, called 'PB

Vallejo', which gave residents the power to decide how to spend 30% of the city's revenue generated by the Measure B sales tax. Over the course of six months, Vallejo residents and stakeholders brainstormed project ideas and developed proposals for a ballot based on those ideas. They had three main goals in mind: 'improve our city, engage our community, and transform our democracy'. Residents volunteered to be delegates, participating in delegate meetings for four months in order to review the ideas from the budget assemblies and develop the best into proposals. Once the proposals were prepared, a Project Expo was held for the community to come back and provide feedback, culminating in a vote by residents in May 2012. Over 4,000 residents aged 16 and older voted on 33 project proposals and the top 12 projects were approved for funding by the City Council. The delegates have remained active in the project to evaluate the process and monitor the implementation of the projects.

CASE STORY

Emily Sadigh's work at the sustainability office at Alameda County, California to engage 9,000 employees in implementing 'green' practices used a set of design principles from nature, such as being locally attuned and responsive, to inform the work of 26 Green Ambassadors. Employees from 10 different county agencies volunteered to act as peer educators in their divisions. They created a person-to-person campaign using innovative ideas to promote carpooling, environmentally responsible purchasing, and other

> workplace choices that supported internal change leadership efforts. Learn more about these efforts at **http://acsustain.org.**

Advances in technology (Skype, conference technology, social network platforms, etc.) and the contributions people like David Rock, author of *Your Brain At Work,* have made to our understanding of neuroscience over the past 10 years have improved our ability to create highly interactive virtual environments, knocking down many of the barriers to engaging larger groups of people. Companies are using interactive methods to create community-built brands, which engage customers in the selection of 'winners' (Super bowl Coke ad, American Idol) or crowdsourcing opinions about what should receive funding or attention. Applying these approaches to building strategic focus around sustainability inside your organization provides a fresh way to engage employees and build internal commitment.

A picture is worth a thousand words

Our brains are constantly constructing maps from multiple pieces of information to help us make sense of the world. Before we had writing, we had stories and pictures which helped us communicate important information. As our use of images becomes more sophisticated and refined with computer-generated graphic images, there is an opportunity to use hand-drawn maps as a way to engage people in co-creating ideas and initiatives where sustainability actions can have an impact.

People use external maps to make sense of changes and identify where they have come from, where they are, and where they are going. Leaders can use this same kind of mapping to demonstrate how sustainability is integrated into organizational strategy and practice. These visual maps can be used to engage people in conversations about how opportunities for sustainability can catalyze efficiency, cost savings, and brand differentiation.

The most compelling maps are co-created as people share information from their experience of sustainability, creating a shared model of reference to identify key leverage points for greater impact.

CASE STORY

When designing how to engage thousands of Walmart employees, a design team was formed with representatives of all groups to be involved (warehouse stockers, cashiers, sales associates, logistics, etc.) in several mapping sessions. During these sessions they identified a shared vision of what the impact of each person identifying their personal sustainability practice (PSP) could represent to the organizations' goals of 1) being supplied 100% by renewable energy; 2) creating zero waste; and 3) selling products that sustain people and the environment. These connections were then translated into a general map of the journey of each store toward its own self-identified goals. As individual associates identified their PSPs, they were encouraged to create images representing their commitments (bulletin board displays, posters, poster displays, peer-to-peer sharing platforms, etc.). These images were gathered in the break rooms, forming a visual affirmation of the diversity and extent of the adoption of self-initiated behavior change.

CASE STORY

The halls at Southwest Airlines are lined with photographs of their employees, and not just employees at work but also employees with their families. This creates a culture where workers feel valued as people, not just as workers. They feel like they are all part of one large family, which carries over into the way employees treat customers like part of that same family. There is an undying loyalty both with employees and customers at Southwest.

Stories anchor sustainability change

Just as with mapping, people naturally tell stories to each other as a way communicating what is important. Our brains create memories, which are webs of connection, not stored in any one specific place in the brain. Successful leaders tell stories to help people create better memories by holding people's attention, giving them an opportunity to connect the new information to what they already know, seeing insights and patterns. Stories engage people's emotions, leaving a more compelling impression than just disembodied lists of facts would.

Sustainability is about personal and organizational actions that make a difference to how people live and work, so stories of what people are doing and the impacts their actions have will connect people to you and engage them with the ideas you are sharing. A story increases the opportunity to inspire thought and action in your listeners.

Compare the difference between these two messages about using reusable bags:

MESSAGE 1: BULLETED LIST

Reusable bags are an excellent way to:

- Cut waste

- Reduce the amount of plastic and chemicals in the environment

- Demonstrate that you are a conscious consumer

Make a difference today by carrying reusable bags with you when you shop!

MESSAGE 2: ELAINE'S STORY

My name is Elaine, and I'm a Resource Center Specialist in the Raleigh office. I started shopping with a reusable bag because my son and daughter told me that it makes a big difference across the spectrum: you reduce waste, keep plastic and chemicals out of the environment, and it doesn't cost anything. At first I'd forget them all the time, but when I did I'd just go back to my car and get those bags. At home I'd unload the groceries and then put the bags back in the trunk right away so I'd have them for next time. It took a few weeks of having to go back to my car, but it didn't take long until I had a new habit!

ELAINE, RESOURCE CENTER SPECIALIST, RALEIGH

Both messages outline the reasons why switching to reusable bags is an environmentally responsible choice, and both offer suggestions for practical steps to take to make the switch. However, Elaine's story is full of details that help listeners connect with her experience. Elaine is a coworker in a close-knit firm, so the reader is more interested in understanding why she cares about using reusable bags. In addition,

Elaine's explanation of how she solved the challenge of remembering her bags addresses an immediate concern of the reader and allows them to imagine how they might take action to tackle that problem themselves.

Telling a good story

A good story does not have to be heroic. Everyday actions can be inspiring and give people encouragement to take steps. A good story should be:

- **Simple.** Each story should convey one main idea.

- **Authentic.** The details should be real and convey your passion.

- **Emotional.** Talk about your feelings, not just the facts.

- **Concrete.** Details make a story more authentic. Talk about time and place.

- **Visual.** Include a picture, map, or other object that serves as a prompt that you can talk to.

....

FIGURE 11. Good stories are simple, authentic, emotional, and concrete.

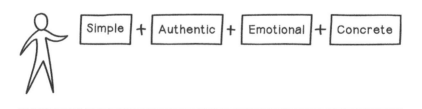

....

How to spot a good story

Good stories are everywhere. Use your cell phone to take pictures of people in action. Anchor people's memories with images and Tweets about what you have just seen.

- **Small steps, big impact.** Tell stories about people doing things that create impact.

- **Best in class.** Tell stories about a person or team setting the bar high for others.

- **Put yourself in the picture.** Use personal examples; include people you have met.

- **Connect to the future.** An important component of the 'sustainability story' is how we impact the future and future generations. Telling stories about how your children, local schools, or community groups are embracing sustainability provides powerful encouragement.

How to document and share stories

In addition to capturing stories, there are a number of ways to document and share:

- Add stories to your briefings and presentations.

- Feature a colleague with a great story in a video and share it.

- Keep a stories journal so you have a source of stories for any situation.

- Create a photo book telling the story of an event or person.

- Mobilize social and other informal networks. Make space for others to comment and share their own stories.

> **CASE STORY**
>
> 2014 will be the 75th anniversary for the American Society for Public Administration (ASPA). To celebrate, ASPA is collecting the stories of public servants to change the conversation about government and public service. The project is titled 'Ask Me Why I Care' and focuses on the service of everyday public servants who usually go unrecognized, highlighting their stories and their motivations for working in public service. For example, Seth Magden responded to Hurricane Katrina by working with FEMA as a housing inspector, but through his one-on-one interviews with the residents of New Orleans and the surrounding parishes, he gained an appreciation for 'why New Orleans matters' and ended up staying on to do hands-on work as a volunteer with Habitat for Humanity before being hired on as the Special Projects Team Lead for the Hazard Mitigation Grant Program.

Steer: Implement and calibrate

This is where the impact and results of the first three actions – sense, scout, and synthesize – manifest. At this point in the change journey, the tension of the S curve often snaps: the tipping point has been reached and it is clear that there is no going back to the prior way of doing things. It can be hard to predict just how this shift will manifest. Leaders of sustainability efforts can think that all the careful planning and set up will lead to action in a smooth and predictable way, but bumps in the road are inevitable. One change creates the opportunity for others to take place in a continuous cycle of mobilizing action, tracking progress, telling impact stories, and giving and using feedback on progress. Leading sustainability efforts take more than one-time action but an ongoing stewardship of bringing sustainability into all levels of organizational life.

Mobilize action

One person's actions can have a powerful effect on others, especially if that person is the leader of their group. Actions can also have the opposite effect if the leader says one thing and does another. Stories and visible actions can have a profound effect on behavior change.

CASE STORY

A senior partner at a prestigious law firm talked about sustainability action as he stood in front of a table overflowing with paper coffee cups to demonstrate how many cups he had been using each month. The visual demonstration of the mound of cups used and disposed of made the clear statement that this kind of waste was no longer acceptable. Using his personal story to show how individual action could make a difference catalyzed others to examine and change their behaviors. The story of this meeting quickly spread among the offices and prompted change in many locations.

Measure and show results

Being able to demonstrate change requires some way of showing the difference being made. This can be in the form of highly specific measurements (for example, tonnes of carbon) or of new behaviors that link to impact metrics (for example, an increase in employee engagement strategies leading to lower turnover).

CASE STORY

A plant manager took one of the plant's monthly utility bills, reproduced it in large banner, and hung it over the cafeteria entrance. It showed a high level of use and cost. It was his way of

---

demonstrating that everyone was responsible for this bill. Being transparent and showing everyone the results of their own behavior sparked a conversation about waste and energy reduction. The resulting ideas were turned into action (turning off lights, shutting down computers, etc.). The bill continued to be hung, displaying the reduced costs to provide a reinforcing reminder of the impact of their actions.

Demonstrate commitment

Systems are very sensitive to change when it is leveraged through the leadership of the organization – a small change can send a powerful signal.

CASE STORY

The new CEO of a hospital wanted to send a dramatic message about being open to new ideas. Her office was in a part of the building that was located behind some beautifully crafted wooden doors. As a symbolic act of declaring her interest in being available, she had the doors removed, allowing access to her reception area. This action sent a message to the organization that her leadership would be different and that a two-way environment was being established.

The flipside of this sensitivity is that perceived disconnect between what is said and what is done can be incredibly disheartening. The alignment of strategy and action is a continuous challenge, especially considering that when declaring change, there will always be a period of time where the stated goals do not match current actions. Leaders can help close this gap by engaging the resisting of the people who must take up new behaviors.

CASE STORY

A corporate headquarters was moving to align their interest in waste reduction and cost efficiency. This headquarters was located in a very hot climate, and one of the special perks for senior managers was to have individual refrigerators filled with bottles of water in their offices. In discussing what leaders could do to model this values shift, it was suggested that senior managers relinquish their refrigerators and use a centralized source of water. A date was set for pickup, but it never occurred: the senior managers were unwilling to release their refrigerators. Their refusal sent the message that it was okay for others to continue their old wasteful habits as well. The inability to experience personal discomfort with the change at hand – the resisting phase – is often responsible for derailing many well-intentioned changes. Because leaders play a very important role in changing behavior, the company's sustainability team held a meeting to engage the senior managers giving them an opportunity to discuss their discomfort with the change. As a result of these conversations, the managers decided that going refrigerator-less was a strong way to model commitment to the organization's sustainability goals. The most senior leader made a big show of having his refrigerator removed, and others did the same. If there had been no opportunity for the senior managers to express their resisting over having to change their patterns, this scenario could have been merely an example of compliance instead of commitment. The discussion prompted the

---

managers to move from resisting to exploring and demonstrate their own willingness to change.

Dealing with unintended consequences

Because all change occurs in a larger system of relationships, there will be times when a well-intentioned change creates unintended consequences in other parts of the system. These are to be expected and anticipated as opportunities for learning about the reach of actions. Taking time to think through all the touch points will give you a broader insight into potential relationships.

CASE STORY

The PSP Project at Walmart was intended to influence the behavior of associates. What ended up happening was an impact on the behavior of their families and friends to take up sustainability-focused actions. This unintended consequence resulted in community clean-ups, school recycling projects, changes in cafeteria food, and sponsorship of recycling facilities.

Continuous learning and relearning

We have discovered that change takes time and is a continuous process, especially as new innovation comes into the picture. Innovation is the result of many approximations; the path forward is not always apparent but emerges as things are tried and refined. Leaders make mistakes, just like all humans do. When you make a mistake, apologize and start over. Sustainability leaders join a long tradition of change agents who tried things before they were proven. Using rapid prototyping and pilots provides a frame for trying things and gaining feedback for modification. Many leaders of these efforts to impact environmental, social, economic, and cultural practices will experience failure, perhaps more than others. This is the cost of innovation at the pace of change that is needed.

Ensure feedback and incorporate learning

The surest way to maintain momentum for any change is to keep learning about how to improve your results and adjusting based on that information. Rapid feedback provides data for rapid improvement and creates an environment of accountability and transparency that fosters innovation. Such environments necessarily include a naturally occurring cycle of pausing to evaluate results, not just at the easily measured level of energy saved, waste diverted, and costs reduced but also at the level of engagement and willingness to go to the next level of change.

The leadership jump

The importance of taking the emotional temperature around the change is often missed, resulting in victory being declared, only to have all the effort slip away. This is related to a phenomenon called 'flight to health' where leaders are fooled by early action and enthusiasm for a change, only to be surprised when people quickly revert to their old behaviors. This occurs when people are pressured to 'get with it' without having been given the time to acknowledge the loss of comfort, pattern or certainty that is being challenged with the change – when they are forced to jump directly from denying to committing. One reason this happens is that leaders generally know about the change far in advance, having been its main architects, and therefore have more control and knowledge regarding the change. This gives them time to go through their own resisting and exploring phases, while employees or other team members are just starting their journey through the Transition Curve.

....

FIGURE 12. The leadership gap occurs when leaders transition ahead of those they are trying to lead.

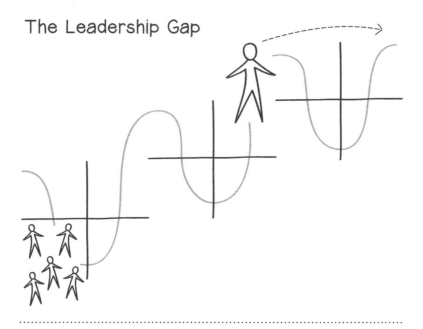

The result is a disconnect between leaders and the people they are trying to lead. In these cases, the solution is to have the leader return to waking people up, identifying and acknowledging their loss of certainty, and supporting and focusing their exploration of options. As we mentioned earlier, not going through the Transition Curve in sequence means having to go back and bring to the surface any unexpressed resisting at the cost of much lost time and effort.

Individual resilience = organizational resilience

In the process of implementation, it is important to remember that building organizational resilience will be an important part of every ongoing commitment and innovation.

Recall the four practices that sustainability leaders use to develop personal resilience – you can use the same four areas to bring resilience to their organizations:

....

FIGURE 13. Coherence, control, challenge, and connection help both individuals and organizations build resilience.

Individual Resilience = Organizational Resilience

Individual Resilience

Organizational Resilience

....

- **Coherence:** Ensure that people in and affected by the organization understand the values, vision, and mission for the sustainability actions. Connect their action to strategy, customer needs and industry leadership.

- **Control:** Help focus enthusiasm on a few things that will provide a focal point for stories. Appreciate what is already working and do more of it.

- **Challenge:** Lead with big goals, inspire action beyond the current level of impact.

- **Connection:** Bring people together to celebrate and acknowledge what they are doing. Gather stories of personal efforts, spread them, encourage micro-action, and look for bottom-up efforts to highlight. Increase voluntary initiative.

....

PART 3

Maintaining Resilience and Agility

LEADING SUSTAINABILITY WORK requires a great deal of emphasis on having a personal alignment with the work you are doing. You don't have to be perfect but you do have to understand how your own personal values connect to your work in the context of sustainability. Taking time to examine how your values and your work are linked, and taking time to address potential disconnects between your actions and your words, will provide resilience and career stamina as you continue to grow and lead as a change agent.

Have a purpose

Very often leadership is focused on building competencies and creating results. An important aspect of sustainability leadership is the opportunity to connect your personal story to what you do. You will be asked over and over why you are doing what you are doing. Your answer will give you a way to remind yourself of your purpose and an opportunity to offer a personal story of why you are involved in this work. It may be as simple as wanting your children and grandchildren to have a thriving world to grow up in or as complex as creating an organization that provides innovative solutions for alternative energy.

Refresh and strengthen your connection to your work by asking yourself these questions at regular intervals:

- Who are you?

- What do you do?

- Why do you matter?

Your answers to these questions will provide the foundation of your resilience and impact as a leader.

Transparency not perfection

An increased emphasis on the connection between your personal choices and leadership actions comes with the territory. If you are advocating change in your organization, you will be watched to see whether you are 'walking your talk'. No one is perfect, and the willingness to receive feedback and provide genuine acknowledgement of others' efforts will go a long way toward establishing an environment of innovation and change. The compassion for how hard it is to make change is a good thing to remember when your behavior falls short. Be mindful of daily choices and be open to acknowledging imperfect alignment of values with behavior.

The ability of leaders to use their own stories of how they have changed their behavior in their personal lives is a powerful leadership opportunity. Using personal examples of how you got through your resisting will provide a model for others to acknowledge their resisting and be able to move forward.

Living in legacy

Sustainability leaders often come to their actions as a result of a transformative personal experiences which caused them to shift the focus of their thoughts and actions from the present to the future. These transformations can come in the form of a health challenge, personal or family experience, or some experience that makes them aware of the magnitude of the impact of their life. These experiences put them into 'legacy' or stewardship thinking, concerned with ensuring or preserving something for the next generation.

CASE STORY

This happened to Lee Scott, former president and CEO of Walmart. When he toured the Amazon basin with Greenpeace and saw the results of deforestation, magnified by his realization that in the wake of Hurricane Katrina, Walmart was among the first responders, even before government resources could be deployed. Following those experiences he began to focus on the impact of changes that Walmart could enact through requiring their suppliers to follow the corporation's sustainability index.

Make sustainability your brand

Sustainability enables you to refresh your career and focus on areas that you have passion for. It provides a new way to direct your talents and capabilities toward an area that is presenting challenges and opportunities to organizations. Having deep experience in sales, marketing, finance, technology, etc., provides a platform for you to see how your area can contribute to broader organizational strategy and internal leadership.

CASE STORY

A senior product manager at Alcatel-Lucent used his 10 years of experience marketing profitable products to leverage a new position as director of sustainability in his organization. He attended the Executive Certificate in Sustainability at Presidio Graduate School to focus his interest and knowledge. As a result of this he became responsible for measuring, reporting, and implementing programs to reduce Alcatel-Lucent's carbon footprint and implement the principles of sustainable management across the organization.

Stay strengths focused

Focus on what is working. Especially when thinking and acting on sustainability issues, it is easy to be focused on what isn't working, what needs to be done, and how big the gap is between current action and sustainable practice. Sustainability leaders need to combine a strong sense of accurate assessment with an ability to keep looking for what is working. This focused attention on the often small ways that things that are changing for the better creates an environment that nurtures innovation and hope. Emphasize the pattern that is taking shape.

This is where telling stories about what people are doing, on the Web and through social media, bulletin boards, newsletters, and posters in the cafeteria or break room, allows others to become inspired by those actions. There is often a concern that the whole story is not there and so leaders or communications departments want to hold back. Letting the story be built makes it more authentic and compelling.

To stay focused on strengths, ask yourself the following questions:

- Where is sustainability making the most impact in my organization?

- Which groups are interested in sustainability action?

The biggest recent shift in leadership research has been the emphasis on building upon your strengths rather than 'fixing' weaknesses. No single model of leadership competencies, styles, traits leads to success; there is no magic bullet. Therefore the best path you can choose is one that focuses on your natural talents, growing your capability in those areas instead of aspiring to a certain set of behaviors.

Preventing burnout

Leaders of sustainability initiatives are change agents, and change agents get burned out because they care. The physical and emotional exhaustion manifests itself in a decreased ability to be effective at what you have always done and a sense of being cut off from yourself and others. Burnout is not changed by long weekends of sleeping or vacations. It signals the need for a reset of life choices and self-care practices.

To prevent wasting your passion for change, revisit the four personal practices that build personal resilience:

- **Coherence:** Revisit your values and appreciate why you do the work you do. Remind yourself of your story and tell it to others.

- **Control:** Start small. Do something to change your everyday behavior. Just keep moving forward.

- **Challenge:** Build on your strengths to stretch yourself. Be curious.

- **Connection:** Seek out other change agents. Nurture relationships. Let people know what you are doing.

Leading for sustainability and change

As our case stories have illustrated, leaders are using a broad set of navigational tools to enhance their personal resilience and stimulate changes in policy and organizational operation in order to meet any number of new challenges that reside under the umbrella of sustainability.

Successful sustainability leaders are masters of a new set of skills. They use their personal values and stories to maintain focus and motivation. They map complex relationships and facilitate among multiple stakeholders, building coalitions of unlikely allies. They focus on what is working to inspire new ways of thinking and generate commitment to behavior change. They structure and maintain their change efforts over long periods of time – they don't give up.

These leaders are simultaneously seeing the interconnection of various systems and translating that perspective into new products, services, and governance models. We wrote this book to inspire new leaders, like you, to make the changes that will turn these ideas into practice....

For Product Safety Concerns and Information please contact our EU
representative GPSR@taylorandfrancis.com
Taylor & Francis Verlag GmbH, Kaufingerstraße 24, 80331 München, Germany

www.ingramcontent.com/pod-product-compliance
Ingram Content Group UK Ltd.
Pitfield, Milton Keynes, MK11 3LW, UK
UKHW040928180425
457613UK00011B/294